DISCOVERY QUESTIONS

Steven Anderson

Discovery Questions by Steven Anderson

Copyright © Steven Anderson 2019

1. Where are you? Genesis 3:9   **7**
2. Why are you angry? Genesis 4:6   **12**
3. Where have you come from, and where are you going? Genesis 16:8   **17**
4. Is anything too hard for the Lord? Genesis 18:14   **22**
5. What is your name? Genesis 32:27   **26**
6. What is that in your hand? Exodus 4:2   **31**
7. What are you doing here? 1 Kings 19:13   **36**
8. Whom shall I send, and who will go for Us? Isaiah 6:8   **41**
9. Can these bones live? Ezekiel 37:3   **45**
10. What do you see? Jeremiah 1:11   **49**
11. Why did you doubt? Matthew 14:31   **54**
12. Why are you afraid? Where is your faith? Mark 4:40   **60**
13. Is your heart still hardened? Mark 8:17   **65**
14. Who do you say that I am? Mark 8:27   **71**
15. What were you arguing about? Mark 9:33 **75**
16. What do you want Me to do for you? Mark 10:51   **80**
17. Are you still sleeping? Mark 14:41   **85**
18. What are you seeking? John 1:38   **91**
19. Do you want to get well? John 5:6   **94**
20. Do you love Me? John 21:17   **98**

Introduction:

"Finding the right questions is as crucial as finding the right answers." Henri Nouwen

Why does the all-knowing God ask questions? It is clearly not so that He can gain information or wisdom from us. His questions to us are for our benefit - to make us think, ponder, pray, search and discover something more about ourselves, about life and about God Himself, and how He wants to interact with us and what He wants to form in us.

We often want to question things, and rightly so at times. We look for answers to the mysteries of life, to the hardships and difficulties it throws in our direction. But what is God asking us? Maybe as we let His questions address us we will discover the most important answers. 'Finding the right questions is as crucial as finding the right answers.' What if we are not asking the best questions?

God's questions are not looking for smart answers or rapid responses? They are designed to stop us, calling us to be still. These questions beckon us to reflect, listening to the depth of our hearts while being led by the Holy Spirit in the light of Christ. They draw us into prayer and a greater understanding; to repentance where we change the way we think; and into new hope, new possibilities and new life.

God's questions can be searching but they are always redemptive. They come from the heart of the Father who loves us and is determined to form us into the likeness of His Son. We may have been used to questions with a different tone though – questions that felt like accusations, or ones that seemed sarcastic, judgemental or condescending. It is important to appreciate the heart of the One asking the question.

As you listen to the Lord asking you these questions as He asked others throughout the Bible, make space and take time to let each question enter your inmost being, exposing your defences, even creating vulnerability before Him. This is the place where we learn to trust Him more and more. Let His questions invite and challenge you to discover new heights and breadths and depths and lengths of what is possible for you in Christ and through the power of His indwelling Spirit.

1. Where are you?

Genesis 3:9

The Lord God came walking in the garden in the cool of the day to meet and commune with Adam. It sounds a most pleasant encounter and appears as a regular practice. But this day something is different, something has fundamentally shifted – and Adam and Eve are hiding.

God is looking for us! He is inviting us into an ever deepening and expanding relationship - a relationship that already exists in the Godhead between Father, Son and Holy Spirit. He is challenging us to enter into the vulnerability of a living relationship when we often would rather abide by the predictability of a set of rules.

He is calling us to live in the immediacy of His Presence - that is into a direct and present involvement with Him. That is the way that Jesus lived. He was one with the Father:

"I and the Father are one" (John 10:30),

And He was always presently doing what He saw the Father doing:

"Whatever the Father does, these things the Son also does in like manner" (John 5:19).

We are being drawn more fully into realising a relationship with no intermediaries where we have direct access to and acceptance in His Presence.

God comes looking and asking – 'Where are you?' It is not with the tone of an angry parent looking for a disobedient child, but that of the Father giving us the opportunity to respond, to come clean and to be restored.

The Presence (Face) and voice of the Lord
This is what we truly long for in the depth of our created being. This is what we need to see and hear, and to be exposed to. (In Hebrew the word for presence and face is the same).
Psalm 16:11 declares:

"In Your presence is fullness of joy."

Then in Psalm 27:4 David articulates his heart's desire: "To behold the beauty of the LORD, and to inquire in His temple."

Numbers 6:24-26 gives us the wonderful blessing of the LORD upon His people whereby His face (presence) might shine upon us. His face and voice are accessible, are beautiful and life-giving in every way – yet we still hide!

Adam and Eve hid thinking the trees of the garden might obscure God's view. To hide, which also means to withdraw, leads us into isolation. So why did they hide? They were afraid, painfully and embarrassingly aware of their nakedness, and feeling the shame of their actions. For the very first time they experienced an acute sense of vulnerability and of being exposed. We can relate to their feelings. Who hasn't felt that fear, that shame or guilt? We feel defenceless and unmasked, and we don't like what others will see. So like Adam and Eve we make coverings of fig leaves. We make feeble attempts to sort ourselves out, only highlighting the weakness and illusion of our self-sufficiency. Many have fallen to that great lie that we need to sort ourselves for God! We think that somehow we need to effect the change before we can come into His Presence. We discover later in this third chapter of Genesis that God makes coverings for Adam and Eve, and much better ones at that. This is all in anticipation of what Jesus Christ brings to us as He gives us a robe of righteousness and invites us to clothe ourselves with Him.

Where are you in relation to God's Presence and voice?

Are you hiding in any way? Are you trying to cover up? Or keep up some sort of pretence? Is any fear keeping you back, and causing you to be withdrawn?

What are your 'fig leaves'? These can even be your service or ministry, or maybe even your spirituality? Maybe you reason that if you pray and read the Bible for an hour then you have got it covered, while the Father is inviting you to be with Him – yes, maybe some praying and reading His Word for sure, but out of the desire for His Presence and voice, not covering yourself but exposing yourself once again to Him.

So will you come to be fully present to Him? Will you come to be fully present in His Presence - moving from any pretence to His Presence? God invites us to a realisation that in Christ we have nothing to fear, nothing to hide, and nothing to prove. His perfect love removes punishment and drives out all fear. His inextinguishable light has already exposed us, bringing the necessary exposure to His Presence that His image may be reformed in us. His fully sufficient sacrifice has made us, by grace, what we could never be by any other means.

Jesus brings us fullness of life where we can live fully present and therefore be fully alive – living in the immediacy of His Presence – to commune, communicate, and be commissioned. He brings us into this relationship with purpose where we hear His voice, where we present ourselves now unafraid and unashamed, that we might carry His Presence to the world.

The Father calls out – where are you? He is inviting, drawing, pursuing, and finding you.

2. Why are you angry?

Genesis 4:6

Two brothers – partners or rivals, co-operating or competing? Many brothers grow up fighting each other yet fighting for each other. Here we find Cain and Abel bringing their offerings to the Lord. They had taken different paths and occupations, one kept sheep while the other tilled the ground. It appears that Abel brought a true sacrifice while Cain merely presented some leftovers or extras. The issue that ensues is due to Abel's offering being accepted - given regard, respect and recognition, while neither Cain nor his offering is given that appreciation and approval. Cain gets very angry and his face falls into a sulk.

God enters the scene with His question: 'Why are you angry?' 'Why' questions look to get to the root. We could ask ourselves, 'What makes me angry?' and come up with a list (maybe a long one!), but the question would still remain, 'Why?'

So, what is anger? A dictionary definition might be 'a strong feeling of annoyance, displeasure or hostility.' The Hebrew term in Genesis is associated with the idea 'hot' and 'to burn,' hence we say to burn with anger. Elsewhere Paul quotes the Psalm which says 'in your anger do not sin,' and then counsels us not go to bed angry thereby giving the devil a foothold in us (Ephesians 4:26-27). When anger is left unchecked and its root unrecognised, then sin crouches at the door looking for its destructive opportunity. (There are different causes and even types of anger too. For example anger at some injustice may be the motivating factor to take righteous action).

God's question is giving Cain a different opportunity; to pause and to examine his heart, and to deal with the cause of his anger. Cain clearly refuses the opportunity but allows his anger to run unbridled and headlong resulting in murder. Jesus also warned of the destructive path that anger can lead us down:

"But I say to you that everyone who is angry with his brother shall be guilty before the court; and whoever says to his brother, 'You good-for-nothing,' shall be guilty before the supreme court; and whoever says, 'You fool,' shall be guilty enough to go into the fiery hell" (Matthew 5:22).

Why are you angry? Maybe you protest and innocently declare that you are not! Yet anger can lay hidden, deep down behind polite and pleasant sounding defences, smiling on the outside but inwardly simmering or even seething. We can be afraid to let anger surface, maybe because we recognise its destructive nature, or not knowing if it will ever stop once vented, or maybe because we are guarding our reputation. Yet in its hiding place in the soul it will silently run rampant bringing about various forms of dis-ease. God's questions continue to challenge and to invite us into His solutions.

Let's get back to the cause of Cain's anger – lack of regard, respect and recognition; and not just that but also that his little brother received all these. Anger comes when things don't go our way, and we measure that often by the supposed successes of others.

God brings us into relationship with Himself where He can bless us to be a blessing. We are designed to live in divine favour. The opposite of blessing is curse which essentially means to hem in, to restrict, and to hinder life from thriving. When that happens we feel frustrated and often get angry. If everyone is in the same boat it might not feel so bad, but when other people are prospering...

So how do we live in the favour of God? Jesus announced the year (time) of God's favour. It's available! Paul gives a clue about acceptable sacrifices calling us to 'present our bodies as a living sacrifice' which he says is 'acceptable to God' (Romans 12:1). Maybe as we abandon our rights to get our own way, and give Him the full rights to our lives, we can enjoy His intended favour. It ceases to be about me getting recognition, but Jesus' life being recognised in me.

So how do we enjoy the favour of God in the midst of unfavourable circumstances? Paul makes an outrageous statement in his letter to the Corinthians about delighting and taking pleasure in a whole load of very unfavourable circumstances:

"Therefore I am well content with weaknesses, with insults, with distresses, with persecutions, with difficulties; for Christ's sake" (2 Corinthians 12:10). Paul hadn't just learned a theoretical idea; he had entered the wisdom of God in a truly participative experience. He had gained a very different perspective. He understood and knew the undercurrent of God's goodness that carried him through every storm.

Why are you angry?
Why do you get offended?
Why does your face become downcast?

When we let go of our rights we gain Christ's inheritance. He was the ultimate and supremely acceptable offering. When we find ourselves accepted and favoured in identification with Him we can stop seeking to be regarded and cease demanding to be respected. We have found true value and affirmation elsewhere, from the very mouth of God. That is enough. God's favour is so infinitely vast that it does not need to be competed for but simply co-operated with, a 'co-operating' that generously releases this favour into a world bruised by the fruit of much anger.

3. Where have you come from, and where are you going?

Genesis 16:8

The Angel of LORD finds a broken, dispirited, pregnant woman, who is fleeing from a place of harsh treatment. Hagar is by a spring in the midst of a desert wilderness. The angel, God's messenger, brings this double question from God to this bewildered young woman. As Hagar is found by God's angel she in turn discovers the 'God who sees' (Genesis 16:13). The One who sees her - sees her plight, her past and her possibilities.

Where have you come from?

You didn't just appear where you are, you came from somewhere. We are affected, indeed largely shaped by our history, as individuals, as communities and even as nations. Out of what soil has your life grown? What has been passed on to you from the generations and what has been handed down to you? These things include the colour of your eyes and hair, and things that can't be changed. It will also include 'narratives' – the stories and sayings that bring understanding of who you are and how to conduct yourself in this world. Some have heard narratives borne out of fear – don't take risks, it's not safe to go there and so on. Others may have received permission giving sayings and attitudes, telling you 'to go for it' and 'nothing ventured, nothing gained.'

What 'narratives' did you grow up with? What formative ideas about life, about who you are, were communicated to you? What is helping and what is hindering?

Where have you come from on your spiritual journey? That walk with God that began maybe before you realised. The Lord is a Shepherd who leads and guides His sheep. The journey can have many stages as it did for Israel and many characters in the Bible. There may be some key moments, encounters with God and His voice. Places where we put up signposts that we can go back and refer to at times. Places where we set up our stones of remembrance to encourage us in difficult times and spiritual droughts. The journey is rarely straightforward, though it does go forward. Often it will contain detours, deserts where we seem to wander in circles, delays that bring frustration and disappointments that could deflect us away from God's purposes. There is lots of preparation! God is always preparing us and setting us up for what's next. He takes us through the seasons of preparation into our greater potential and purpose.

In what ways is your future direction being determined by your past? There may be both positives and negatives in your answer. Recognising our heritage can help us to more fully embrace and benefit from it. Being aware of the hindering factors of our history can enable us to find the way to break free from their clutches and confines.

Where have you come from? A question worth sitting with, pondering and praying over and letting the Holy Spirit bring clarity to what we should be thankful for and what we may need to find release from. That release will come through the grace and truth that Jesus comes revealing to us. He generously dispenses grace to forgive (even ourselves) and grace to accept what can't be changed. He abundantly reveals truth that exposes the lies and half-truths that we have believed, the truth that sets us free to believe God's word.

Where are you going?

God took David from following the sheep to leading the nation. God takes people from humble, small beginnings and calls them forward into the significance of serving Him on a road with endless possibilities.

So where are you going? Any idea? No idea? Clear plans and goals?

Whatever our present understanding, the truth is that God's intention is to take us forward in His 'upward call' (Philippians 3:14). Paul had a great religious heritage but it had become a hindrance to knowing Christ. So he let it go, broke free from it and embraced this new life in identification with Christ.

God's call to each one of us is first a call to come to Him, entering into an ever deepening relationship. Out of relationship comes resource and responsibility to give what we have received. His call sets us in motion as something begins to stir inside us even though we may not yet understand it. Sometimes we think we have a handle on it only to discover later how far off we were. He calls from His perspective of completion for us to participate in making that happen. Our view is very partial but as we take each obedient step the purposes of God unfold more and more.

Jesus reveals the ultimate origin and destiny. Before washing His disciples' feet, the Scripture tells us that Jesus knew 'that He had come from God and was going to God' (John 13:3). He lived in the perfect security and significance of Who He was, where He was from and where He was going. A past, present and future all rooted in relationship with His Father, the God who was, and is and is to come.

Our ultimate origin was in the mind of God who knew us before we were born (Psalm 139:13-16). Our ultimate destiny is in the One who has destined us to be conformed into the image of Christ Jesus (Romans 8:29), and to share in His inheritance (Romans 8:17).

4. Is Anything Too Hard for the LORD?

Genesis 18:14

It had been quite an adventure and God had blessed Abraham in many ways. But the big one hadn't happened. God had promised him a son and through him many countless descendants but the promise remained unfulfilled; the reason for his name change from Abram, 'exalted father,' to Abraham, 'father of a multitude.' Being an exalted father is all about you, but a father of a multitude is all about legacy and what you release into the world. The extra letters in his name made a world of a difference.

Yet Abraham had believed God and Paul tells us that 'he did not waver in unbelief but grew strong in faith' (Romans 4:20). But still he and his wife Sarah waited, and grew older, very much older! The promise had reached the point where it couldn't be fulfilled by natural human means. It was like God said, "I am still going to give you a child through Sarah, but it's now reached the point where it is so beyond your ability that it can only happen by My doing."

So God visits Abraham and Sarah's tent in the form of three men. The elderly couple put themselves out to provide the best of hospitality. In the conversation that follows, the long awaited promise is given its final countdown - one year from now. Abraham is reminded, he still believes, his heart stirs afresh. Sarah laughs! It's incredulous! Maybe her laughter is from embarrassment, or she thinks it's too ridiculous. Human reasoning and their experience would loudly declare that this is impossible. So our next question comes to this aged pair, but is mainly directed to the ears of Sarah: 'Is anything too hard for the LORD?'

It is a question to challenge our unbelief and at the same time to extend to us an invitation into greater faith. It is a question that confronts our understanding and definition of what is possible. It is a question that assaults our settings of what is attainable.

Is anything too hard for the LORD?
'Anything' can also have the meaning of any word or speech. The word for 'hard' means beyond one's power to do, difficult to understand, or wonderful and extraordinary. Sarah conceiving and giving birth to a son would be all of these. But if God is who He says He is then what could be beyond His power? Psalm 33:9 says:

"He spoke, and it was done; He commanded and it stood fast".
Therefore anything that God speaks is possible!

Jesus said, 'All things are possible to him who believes' (Mark 9:23). This statement comes in the midst of an episode where Jesus addresses various levels of unbelief – in a father, among a group of His disciples, and even amid a whole generation. We might say that everything that God says is possible to whoever has faith to take Him at His word and believe.

What has God said to you? What do you believe He has promised? What are you facing that seems humanly impossible to solve? Let this question give you hope. Let it stir up faith. Let it confront your definitions of what could be. Let it move the limitations formed by previous experience. Don't let your past experience determine the possibilities of today and tomorrow.

When Jesus is encountered by two blind men who cry out to him for mercy (Matthew 9:27-29), He asks them a similar question: 'Do you believe that I am able to do this?' The men, who have followed Jesus down the road and into the house He entered, displaying determination for men who can't see by themselves, answer affirmatively, 'Yes, Lord.' Jesus touches their eyes, restoring their sight, while declaring that it is according to their faith that this is done.

Jesus is on a search for faith – simple faith, taking God at His word and believing. Where there is faith He can release something from heaven on the earth. Unbelief seems to be one of the biggest obstacles. Indeed in His hometown Jesus couldn't perform any miracles and 'He marvelled because of their unbelief' (Mark 6:6).

However He does not come rebuking our lack of faith, scolding and dismissing us. Instead He asks a question as He did to Sarah and Abraham – a question to make us think. He asks a question to invite us to think beyond our limits, beyond our understanding, and beyond our experience. He asks a question to help us to ask for more than we imagined possible.

Is anything too hard for the LORD? For the One who is risen and has overcome death, and who is seated far above every name, power, dominion and authority?

Whatever He has said, whatever He has promised – do you believe He is able to do this?

5. What is your name?

Genesis 32:27

Jacob was going through quite a crisis! He had been away from home for a considerable length of time but now God had told him to return to the land of his birth (Genesis 31:13). That meant facing his past, his deception, his brother!

Jacob, with some help from his mother, had tricked his brother Esau out of his father's blessing as the firstborn (see Genesis 27). Though Esau was partly to blame due to his careless attitude - he was not at all pleased. He swore revenge and planned to kill his brother, so Jacob fled for his life. Now Jacob is returning and knows he will have to face his brother, facing up to the consequences of his past actions and deceit.

Jacob heads back with his two wives, two female servants and eleven sons. Esau arrives on the scene with 400 men! If there was going to be a fight then it looked like there would be only one possible outcome. Jacob is terrified. He needs a plan. He needs help. So he sends his family ahead and gets alone with God. There follows a bizarre encounter where Jacob wrestles with a man, who turns out to be the Angel of the Lord, who represents the very presence and face of God. In the midst of this wrestling match, Jacob demands a blessing. If there was one thing Jacob understood it was the power of blessing. He tricked his way into getting the best blessing from his father, and now he hangs on, wrestling for God's blessing.

What is your name?

In response to Jacob's desire to be blessed the angel asks him his name. Not that he didn't know but because something transformational was about to take place. He is asking Jacob, 'What have you been called? Who have you been up to now?

What is your name? What are you called? By whom? What do you call yourself? What 'names' have been spoken over you? What effect and even power have those 'names' had over your life and over how you see yourself?

We used to say in the school playground that 'sticks and stones may break my bones, but names will never hurt me.' Not really true! As we grow up and interact socially we are discovering more about who we are. There may be good, affirming names spoken over us, but there are also damaging ones. What 'names' were spoken over you?

A New Name

Jacob gets a new name, Israel. It has various meanings within it – Prince with God, God contends, and one who prevails with God. It would become the name of his nation. Jacob on the other hand meant 'one who grabs the heel' (Genesis 25:26), which figuratively meant a deceiver. Jacob had lived up to his name more than once!

Deception can lurk in every human heart, as Jeremiah declared, 'the heart is deceitful above all things' (Jeremiah 17:9a). The underlying selfishness and fears that drive us to try to get our own way can subtly be at work within us all. Jacob gets a new name which leads to a new way. No longer will he need deception and trickery to get blessed and to prosper. Now he can find blessing God's way.

The meeting with Esau goes better than could ever have been imagined. There is no talk of revenge; there is no violence or threat. Quite the opposite happens as Esau runs to Jacob, embraces him, kisses him and weeps with him. Jacob required no tricks this time, but benefits from the favour of God on his life.

One day Jesus encountered a man called Nathanael. Jesus 'named' him 'a true Israelite in whom there is no deceit' (John 1:47). A compliment indeed! God has better plans and ways for us than we would work out and connive for ourselves. He has a better name for us.

Names changers can really be game changers. Jacob understood this better than most men. Indeed as his final son is born, the baby's mother, Rachel, cries out in pain as she tragically dies. So she names the child Ben-Oni meaning son of my sorrow. However Jacob quickly changes his son's name to Benjamin, son of my right hand. Benjamin could have been named as a reflection of his mother's pain and sorrow. How easily other people can name and define us out of their own issues and pain.

What new name might God have for you?
Naming in the Bible is all about identity and definition. Who am I? This is the deep cry of many hearts. We cannot discover our identity in isolation but in relationship. So parents give names, and do so for all sorts of reasons. God the Father truly names us all as Paul states:

"I bow my knees before the Father, from whom every family in heaven and on earth derives its name" (Ephesians 3:14-15).

He calls forth our true identity in relationship with Him, in Christ. He sets the definition of who we are and thereby what we can accomplish. It is one thing to read about and hear others talk about our identity in Christ; it quite another thing to receive the revelation from God Himself of who He says you are.

Naming and Blessing

Jacob got a new name, and a really good and powerful one at that. He also received a fresh blessing. Naming and blessing go together. To bless is to speak well of someone; to speak words that bring forth a thriving of life, prospering, and purposefulness. This blessing is more than 'just words' or wishful thinking, but when given in the Lord is a spiritual impartation that carries the weight of His favour conveyed by His Holy Spirit.

Where the names spoken over you have restricted and hindered, God is speaking a new name that releases His favour, His increase, and His intention for you.

6. What is that in your hand?

Exodus 4:2

Moses was born during a dangerous and turbulent season. Pharaoh had ordered the death of any Hebrew boys born at this time, but Moses had an eventful and miraculous escape. There was a great destiny in the Lord lying before him and the enemy had sought to eliminate him. While God's hand was with Moses, when he was older he allowed his own hands to get himself into trouble as he slays an Egyptian for beating a Hebrew slave. Found out and fearing for his life, Moses flees into exile and into the wilderness.

We find Moses in the desert, the back of beyond, looking after his father-in- law's sheep. Not exactly the destiny of a great leader, but the necessary training ground. His days may have been largely uneventful: watching the grazing flocks, looking for new pasture, and keeping an eye out for danger. Then one day God breaks in to Moses' life. A burning bush that is not consumed, God calling out his name, and an incredible conversation where God promises deliverance for the

Hebrews and that He's going to bring this about through Moses.

Moses is startled and afraid. He may be thinking, 'Is this for real?' Has God got the right person? Doubts, excuses and questions flood his mind. He feels unqualified and very vulnerable at the thought of going back and speaking to the Hebrews. What if they don't believe him? Will they listen to him? What if they think Moses made up this whole encounter with the living God?

In response to these questions God asks a very simple question. He doesn't give some great statement or justify His choice of Moses, but asks him, 'What is that in your hand?' And Moses gives a very simple answer, 'a staff.' It wasn't anything special, it was something he used every day as a shepherd. Some pretty miraculous stuff follows as this staff becomes a snake and then back into a staff – the ordinary becomes extraordinary.

What is that in your hand?
What are you holding? What have you been given and entrusted with?
We can be so conscious of and concerned about what we don't have that we fail to see the possibilities of what we do have.

Jesus asked a similar question to His disciples one day
(Mark 6:33-43). There was a massive crowd in a
deserted place, the back of beyond, with nothing to eat
and time was going on. Jesus was training and raising up
some leaders who would lead people into freedom just
like Moses. He uses the opportunity to challenge them
to a greater level of faith, suggesting strongly: 'You give
them something to eat.' Like Moses these guys have
questions. Jesus answers with a question: 'How many
loaves do you have?' What is that in your hand?
What is in *your* hand? Begin to look and see. And begin
to see what this could become when it is empowered by
the Lord.
What is God calling you to?
Are you waiting until you get more qualified?
Are you waiting for other people to join you?
Have you questions and doubts? Are you making
excuses? Do you think God has got the wrong person?

What do you think God could do with that which is in your hand?
Moses staff will be used to demonstrate the power of
God over Egypt and all her magicians. This staff will be
used in parting a sea and winning a battle. Moses will

take this ordinary shepherd's staff with him wherever he goes.

Those few loaves and a couple of fish will feed 5,000 men plus women and children. More importantly, Jesus' disciples have participated in a faith stretching miracle. A little while later they face a similar situation (Mark 8:1-10). Again Jesus asks His followers, 'How many loaves do you have?' Sounds familiar – we've heard that question before. Slightly smaller crowd, just 4,000 men plus women and children and there's two more loaves! But still needs a massive miracle to feed them all. The disciples are learning about what is in their hands and what God can do with that.

'Hand' in the Bible is also figuratively a symbol of strength or power. The disciples would come to understand what more was in their hands; the very anointing and power of Christ.

"And through the hands of the apostles many sign and wonders were done among the people" (Acts 5:12).

What is that in your hand? What has been freely given to you in Christ?

The important thing is to believe what God can do with this, and to release what you have under His Spirit's anointing and see what might happen.

7. What are you doing here?

1 Kings 19:9, 13

Elijah bursts onto the scene announcing a drought! This was not the sort of prophetic pronouncement to gain popularity. King Ahab would refer to him as the 'troubler of Israel.'
Elijah's life has some real ups and downs. He goes from victory to collapse.

After announcing a drought in the land, he experiences God's miraculous provision, raises a dead boy back to life, wins an amazing contest when vastly outnumbered by his opponents, and finally calls forth the much needed rains upon the parched land. At this point he seems to be at the top of his game, yet we soon find him on the run. A threat from Queen Jezebel sends Elijah over the edge. He had courageously confronted hundreds of the prophets of Baal. He had stood firm in faith, calling down fire from heaven, and calling the people back to worship the Lord their God. However, all that appears forgotten at the sound of the intimidating voice of an enemy.

The threat was told to him but the Scripture says 'he saw' (1 Kings 19:2-3). He paid attention to the threat; it got in his sights rather than his eyes being on the God of provision and power. He lost focus and he fled for his life. He and his servant got out of there, but then Elijah leaves his servant and flees further. He wants and needs to get alone.

Maybe Elijah was just plain exhausted from the fight and has a bit of a breakdown. He very quickly goes from victory and vindication to fatigue and futility. In the story we see a repeated situation playing out with Elijah. Earlier he had gone to a widow who was on the brink of starvation and was ready to give up and die. Elijah brought her into the experience of the supernatural realm that he had himself known of God's miraculous provision. Now Elijah is the one with the death wish, and this time it is an angel that comes and supplies food for him. Strengthened by the food and re-energised by some sleep Elijah continues his journey until he gets to Mount Horeb where he shelters in a cave. Here God speaks to him and asks the question, 'What are you doing here?'

Twice God will ask Elijah the same question and twice Elijah will give the exact same response:

"I have been very zealous for the LORD,
the God of hosts; for the sons of Israel have forsaken
Your covenant, torn down Your altars and killed Your
prophets with the sword. And I alone am left; and they
seek my life, to take it away" (1 Kings 19:9-10, 13-14).
What do we see in his response? He is feeling sorry for
himself as self-pity has laid its deceptive claim on his
soul. He falls into the classic blame game – it's the
children of Israel's fault – and seeks to justify himself.
The Lord does not engage with Elijah's claims but twice
instructs him to move - 'go out' (v11) and 'go, return'
(v20).

But what about the question? What are you doing here,
Elijah? The implication of the question appears to be
that Elijah is not where he is meant to be. Yet God
meets him in his state of disorientation, disillusionment
and despair, not to scold and not to sympathise either,
for neither will help, but to enable Elijah to re-orientate
and re-focus.

Sometimes we feel we've had enough, other times we
are simply exhausted - we're spent. Sometimes we have
lost our way somewhere on the journey. So the
question comes to us: What are you doing here? Are
you running away from something - maybe a threat or

maybe a responsibility? Have you fallen prey to self-pity, blaming and excusing?

Are you where you are meant to be?
Why are you where you are?
How did you get there?
What are you doing there?
Is this where you want to be?
If not, then what is necessary to move you?

The Lord meets with Elijah in that place, on the mountain. He brings fresh revelation, not in dramatic form but a still, small voice. He gives Elijah a renewed purpose and perspective. He reveals to the prophet that he is not alone but that there are indeed 7000 who have not bowed the knee to Baal. The clutches of self-pity are loosening and fresh motivation is returning. Elijah comes out of his hiding place, out from his paranoia-producing isolation, and receives new instructions and strategy for the next stages of battle.

The Lord is saying to Elijah that he is not alone, that He has not finished with him, and that it is time to return and to raise up others who will help finish the task. He will call up and anoint for purpose a king, a warrior and his own successor as prophet in the land of Israel. Elijah wasn't finished but was entering a new phase. Disorientation will precede reorientation, and a new phase of calling may well be preceded by some sort of crisis.

Elijah felt like giving up but God hadn't given up on him. You may go through similar times where everything seems futile, where giving up seems the easiest option. But God has refreshment and a renewed perspective and purpose for you.

8. Whom shall I send, and who will go for Us?

Isaiah 6:8

Encounters with the living God are always special and life-changing. Isaiah's experience as described in chapter six is one of the most awesome God encounters ever. Heaven's throne is unveiled to him with all its glory, power and majesty. It is an encounter that completely undoes Isaiah, where he feels ruined and devastated in the presence of God's holiness and glory. Yet in the midst of this, he finds cleansing and receives a commissioning.

This episode was set at a particular time - an opportune season. It was the year that King Uzziah died. He had had a long and prosperous reign, but this led to pride when he became over confident in his own strength: "But when he became strong, his heart was so proud that he acted corruptly, and he was unfaithful to the LORD his God" (2 Chronicles 26:16).
So it was with the death of this long-reigning king that Isaiah has this incredible encounter with the ever-reigning King of Kings.

Before getting to God's question there is a powerful prelude preparing Isaiah's heart and understanding. We must never underestimate the importance of preparation as God prepares the ground of our heart and positions us to hear and respond. Isaiah experiences a revelation of the Lord as he sees Him enthroned, and sees and hears the worship of the angelic beings in heaven. It is so powerful that the doorposts shake and the building is filled with smoke at the manifestation of the glory of God.

How would you react to such an explosive encounter with God? Isaiah is blown apart! He cries out that he is ruined, undone, gone to pieces. He is overwhelmingly aware of his uncleanness, particularly that of his lips, his speech. Not only that his lips are unclean but that he also lives among a people of unclean lips. Neither he nor anyone else is ready and in a right condition to speak on behalf of the Lord.

Simon Peter has a similar response when he is confronted with the wonder of Jesus and a miraculous catch of fish:
"But when Simon Peter saw that, he fell down at Jesus' feet, saying, 'Go away from me Lord, for I am a sinful

man!' For amazement had seized him and all his companions because of the catch of fish which they had taken" (Luke 5:8-9).

Jesus doesn't go away from Simon as the fisherman suggested, but in fact uses the experience to call him up to something greater. Isaiah likewise receives God's solution – a burning coal from the altar touching and purging his lips – making him ready to be a mouthpiece for a greater purpose.

In order to be ready to enter into the greater purposes of God we may need to be 'undone' of what we have built and become. Encounters with the glory of God will ruin us for anything less. But here God's touch takes away the false and cleanses the contaminations readying us to function on a higher plane.

Isaiah now 'eavesdrops' on a heavenly conversation overhearing this double question:

Whom shall I send, and who will go for Us?

God is looking for partners, for those whom He can send. He is a sending God – He sent His Son into the world, He sends forth His Spirit, He sends His apostles who are literally the 'sent ones.' He is still asking this question.

Are you listening in on heaven's conversations?

Are you being readied to participate?

Are you prepared to go wherever that might be?

Unlike the other questions we've looked at this one wasn't directed to a specific individual; it was simply asked among the Godhead. Isaiah's attention had been dramatically caught; he was listening, he was available, and he was willing. Sometimes God throws out questions and opportunities. Those who have allowed themselves to be prepared – undone from their own sense of qualification, and ruined for anything less than the purposes of God – are positioned to respond.

9. Can these bones live?

Ezekiel 37:3

Ezekiel's life was characterised by the hand of the Lord coming on him, catching him up in the Spirit and revealing visions to him. It also featured some peculiar prophetic actions that Ezekiel was instructed to do. One day, once again the Lord's hand came upon Ezekiel; he is caught up by the Spirit of God and lands in a valley full of bones. He was by this time probably getting used to these strange experiences. God causes Ezekiel to have a good look around, and the prophet observes that there were very many bones and that they were very dry. It is definitely not a hopeful situation, but one of death and decay. Into these gloomy and gruesome circumstances God poses a question to Ezekiel: 'Can these bones live?'

God's questions are to make us ponder and pray, and to invite and challenge us to something greater. Ezekiel however gives an immediate and clever response – 'O Lord God, You know.' Indeed God does know, but He doesn't want His prophet to opt out but to involve him in what is to come.

However, the question must have struck Ezekiel, and a sense of possibility and faith start to rise up within him. When God instructs him to prophesy to the bones – a seemingly ridiculous thing to do – he obeys as commanded resulting in the dry bones coming together and flesh covering them. There was just one thing lacking, breath. Ezekiel prophesies once more as instructed and the breath of life blows in resulting in a vast army rising up.

Can these bones live? Can that which seems to be dead, even decayed, live again? Can it not only live again but become something powerful? Can a seemingly hopeless situation be turned around?

God was showing Ezekiel a picture of His people, Israel (Ezekiel 37:11-14). They seemed like dry bones, having lost hope and appearing cut off from God. Yet through His prophetic spokesman the Lord was calling His people out of their 'graves' and back to their land and their inheritance.

What might appear as dry bones, void of a sense of hope and appearing to be cut off from God's life and purpose? Yet God asks, 'Can these bones live?' He invites and challenges us to look, and then look again.

He calls us to believe once more. Then He invites us into faith inspired participation, to begin to speak to and prophesy over those 'bones.' He challenges us to join Him in 'calling those things that are not as though they were' (Romans 4:17).

There appears to be three stages of raising the bones back to life and purpose. First, there is a coming together, a connecting up of bone to bone. This can represent an alignment of people or of ministry gifts. The word for 'equip' in the New Testament was used for the concept of resetting and realigning bones. God wants to bring His people into life-giving relationships and into purposeful connections that enable a meaningful and effective working together.

Second, there is a covering of sinew, flesh and skin. These constitute the human body and the Body of Christ with Him as the head:
"From whom the entire body, being supplied and held together by the joints and ligaments, grows with a growth which is from God" (Colossians 2:19).
We are parts of something greater in Christ's body, supporting one another and functioning together, and all covered and clothed in His righteousness.

The third, and most important stage is still to come, and indeed the first two are of no value without the third. The breath of life, the wind of the Spirit must blow and fill these bodies that they may truly live. All the good connections and even great structures, useful as they are, are of no true value unless enlivened and empowered by the Holy Spirit.

Maybe it is a vision or a dream that needs to come together and come to life. Maybe it is your life. Maybe it is a local church or some other work or ministry. Can these bones live? The answer may be, 'O Lord God, you know' but the answer also appears to be 'yes.' That which has fallen apart can come back together. That which has been stripped can be clothed once more. That which has lost its very breath can live again.

10

What do you see?

Jeremiah 1:11, 13

It is amazing that even with their natural eyes two
people can look at the same scene and see quite
different things. One may fail to notice details that
appear clear to the other. It is even more so in how we
interpret what we see. Accounts of what eye witnesses
have seen may vary widely!

God called and raised up Jeremiah as a prophet in a
particularly difficult time. He 'ordained him a prophet to
the nations' (1:5), setting him apart from his mother's
womb, and calling him to function from his youth. As
the Lord begins to move upon Jeremiah, He twice asks
this question of him: What do you see? Jeremiah sees
and the Lord gives him understanding of what this
means. The prophet sees the revelation but also needs
the wisdom to understand what it means and what he is
to do with it.

In asking this question God is looking for those who
display an observant spirit. Moses, a great leader and

also a prophet, noticed a burning bush. This doesn't sound too remarkable in a hot desert. Indeed it was not, but Moses notices that this particular bush despite being aflame is not consumed. He observes something unusual and goes for a closer look. God meets him there and issues the great call to deliver Israel from the land of Egypt.

God is issuing a repeated call to His people to see and to behold, not just glancing at but taking note. Behold – look, observe, study, take note, and ask questions. God wants us to see and then see from His viewpoint. We mustn't be like most of Israel in the time of Isaiah who were ever seeing but never perceiving (Isaiah 6:9-10).

There are different types of sight – hindsight might save us from many mistakes but never comes in time. Then there is insight – an ability to see into and to discern meaning. There is also foresight – an ability to see beyond the present situation or circumstances, to see what is coming and to prepare appropriately. To be people of true vision we need to develop the latter two of these sights.

How do we become people of vision?
On a number of occasions Jesus brought sight to those who were blind, fulfilling promises and prophecy from

the Old Testament. One time the blind man Jesus touches doesn't immediately receive clear sight, but when Jesus asks him what he sees, he replies that he sees 'men like trees walking' (see Mark 8:22-25). Jesus put His hands on the man a second time, resulting in full and clear vision being restored. Maybe you see but it's all a little blurred. Maybe you can't make much sense of what God might be showing you. Maybe things don't look like you think they should. It is time for a fresh touch from Jesus, one that releases sight and vision.

Paul prays for the church in Ephesians 1:17-18:
"That the God of our Lord Jesus Christ, the Father of glory, may give to you a spirit of wisdom and revelation in the knowledge of Him... that the eyes of your heart may be enlightened."
As we keep receiving this, our inner eyes will be trained by the Spirit of God to see the things God is revealing, and as we look and observe and seek wisdom more will become clear. The more we use our spiritual eyes the more we will get spiritual things into focus.

When the Apostle Paul was in Lystra he saw a crippled man who was in the crowd listening to him preaching. Paul 'observed him intently and saw that he had faith to be healed' (Acts 14:9). Paul didn't just see him in the natural, or notice how crippled he was. Paul observed intently, paying full attention to and focus on this man, and saw that the man had faith. How can you see that someone has faith to be healed? You might hear something they say that suggests this, but it appears Paul 'saw' something beyond what natural sight reveals.

One day the prophet Elisha was surrounded by an enemy army. He wasn't too fussed or concerned but his young servant got in quite a state. Elisha prayed, 'open his eyes that he might see' (2 Kings 6:17). The young man's inner eyes were opened, and he saw heaven's army of horses and chariots of fire all around Elisha. I imagine he felt quite reassured.

What do you see?

What do you see that is, and what do you see that could be?

What possibilities and opportunities do you see?

What do you see in the natural realm and what might you see in the spiritual realm?

Jesus said that He only did what he saw the Father doing (John 5:19).

What do you see the Father doing? In your life? Around about you?

Look, observe, study, take note and ask questions.

We are often unconsciously governed by the familiar, only seeing what we expect to see or desire to see. God wants to lead us on new paths, to new things, and to give us a new perspective. His question – What do you see? – is a question that is calling out to us, inviting and challenging us to be a people of true vision.

11
Why did you doubt?
Matthew 14:31

It was the darkest hour of the night, the disciples' boat was being battered and tormented by the waves, and the wind was driving against them. These men were straining at their oars and getting nowhere fast. Jesus, on the other hand, was on a mountain top alone with His Father in prayer surrounded by the peace and presence of heaven.

Jesus sees them and comes to them walking on the sea. He seems to be able to walk quicker than they can row in the midst of the storm. A stress filled situation now becomes filled with fear as the disciples cry out in terror thinking that they are seeing a ghost! As often with the sudden appearances of the Lord, Jesus speaks out words of reassurance seeking to silence the debilitating sound of fear.

Peter, coming to a realisation that it actually is Jesus, makes what is a bold request even for him: "Lord, if it is You, command me to come to You on the water." Jesus answers with one word, "Come!" Peter takes one faith-filled, incredible step out of the boat. He actually does walk on the water! He amazingly begins to move towards Jesus ...but...something else comes in to play. He becomes aware once more of the wind and it's powerfully disruptive and disturbing effects upon the waters, and fear enters into his heart. Sinking into the depths Peter calls out once more to Jesus but this time in desperation. Jesus, taking hold of and rescuing him, asks the question: 'Why did you doubt?'

What is doubt?

There are different words that are translated as 'doubt' in the New Testament. One describes the inner dialogue that goes on in our minds, and another contains the idea of making distinction and separating. The one used here in Matthew basically means 'twice' signifying being in two minds.

Doubt should not be equated with or confused with unbelief. Unbelief is a position taken; a stand that won't believe or refuses to believe. It is what keeps us from God and receiving His redemptive purposes for our lives. If someone is in unbelief then they can't doubt as they have no faith in which to doubt. You can't doubt unless you first have faith. You can't begin to sink unless you first get out of the boat. Peter believed and therefore stepped out, and then doubt came in. Jesus described Peter as 'you of little faith' not 'no faith.'

Why did you doubt?
This question is an invitation to explore the reasons behind our thoughts and actions:
Why did Peter doubt?
Why have you doubted God and His Word in certain situations?
What inner dialogue goes on inside your head?
What were the two minds that you got caught between?
What did you see and focus on that distracted you from the words of Jesus to you?

When Jesus invites and challenges us to go beyond, abundantly beyond, what we would naturally think or even imagine, then this dialogue of two modes of thinking arises within us. His question is not an angry rebuke, but rather an appeal and an encouragement drawing us into greater faith. If we understand why we doubt then we can address this and move forward. It is important that we learn more about ourselves through times of doubt.

How do we overcome doubt and grow in faith?

Peter lost his focus on Jesus – on His ability, the One who was already walking on the water, and on His permission, call and command – 'come!' The wind and waves were powerful and dangerous but the word of Jesus was and is greater than any wind that blows or waves that batter against us. We must always be more impressed with Jesus.

Peter had the greater opportunity to grow because he took the step of faith and risk. The other disciples remained relatively safe in the boat, but in that place the deep impact of this incident would not touch them as it did Peter. Indeed Peter more often than any other of the twelve kept stepping out and sometimes putting his foot in it! Yet through his temporary fallings and failings he found restoration, new opportunities and flourished. A few fallings and failings are part of this faith journey and don't define us. We get up and go on, learning lessons and regaining focus.

So if doubting is being in two minds, causing us to hesitate and to listen to thoughts that question and oppose what God's Word is to us, then a way forward would be to become single minded. That doesn't mean we never question anything or think things through. But there are questions that feed fear and increase doubt, and there are questions that seek understanding and increase faith.

Jesus spoke of the eye being the lamp of the body (Matthew 6:22). He said if the eye is 'single' (KJV) then our whole body will be full of light. The word translated 'single' also means clear or healthy, leading to uncluttered and unobscured vision. If Peter's eye had been single then he would have only seen and been solely focused on Jesus and not the wind and waves.

When Peter was in the boat he saw Jesus. He thought, 'If Jesus is walking on the water then I can too'. Yes he floundered and struggled but Jesus lifted him up for another day. On other occasions Peter would watch Jesus, and seeing what His Lord did, he would think to himself, 'If Jesus can do that so can I'. That was always the message Jesus was trying to get through to His followers. Peter overcame doubt and just as he witnessed Jesus healing the sick so did he. He even followed Jesus' very example as he raised someone from the dead:

"But Peter sent them all out and knelt down and prayed, and turning to the body, he said, 'Tabitha, arise.' And she opened her eyes, and when she saw Peter, she sat up." (Acts 9:40, see Mark 5:37-42). When we press through doubt, not giving it a place of influence in our thinking, we can go and do abundantly beyond!

12

Why are you afraid?

Mark 4:40

It was evening and was getting dark when we find the disciples once again in a boat on the lake. This time Jesus is with them in person, and it is He who has suggested that they cross over to the other side. Suddenly a ferocious storm breaks out all around them with the wind howling about them and the waves crashing against and over into the boat. They are in serious danger. Meanwhile, Jesus is asleep with His head on a pillow in the stern of the boat.

How did these disciples feel? Some were experienced fishermen who knew the waters well. They had likely faced similar situations before. But experience wouldn't save them. They were thrust into a place of deep vulnerability where they lost any sense of security and of being in control. It is often in those times that we learn some of the deepest lessons about ourselves, about life and about our God.

So who or what caused the storm? God? The devil? Natural circumstances? What are the causes and purposes of the storms that we encounter? Our answers to these questions will go a long way to determining our response in the storm. From this passage it seems there are three different responses the disciples could have made:

1.   Wake Jesus – shouting help!
2.   Rebuke the storm themselves.
3.   Sleep and rest through the storm.

They chose the first while Jesus seemed to be engaging in the third response, while maybe He was hoping that His young crew might be bold enough to do the second one! Having been wakened by His panicky followers, and having stilled the wind and waves, Jesus now takes the opportunity to ask two questions:

Why are you afraid? How is that you have no faith?

Why are you afraid?

So what is Jesus actually asking, and wasn't it a bit unfair to ask men who feared for their very lives such a question? The word most commonly used for fear (phobos) is not used here but a word that means fear in the sense of timidity. We might rephrase the question: Why are you intimidated by this storm? Why did you let the sounds and sights of the storm make you so timid that you could take neither take any action nor exercise any faith?

We can be intimidated by many things – the size of a problem, the appearance of an enemy or even the apparent confidence of other people. Goliath sought to intimidate the armies of Israel and succeeded until a young shepherd called David came along who was more impressed with the size of His God than the might of this giant of a man. So what intimidates you? Why? Why are you fearful?
Jesus doesn't ask the disciples what they are afraid of. The answer to that would not have been the storm itself but what they thought was going to be the consequence of this storm - that they were going to die. It is the fear of death that enslaves people in its grip.

In the New Testament, the root of fear is exposed and dealt with by the love and power of God in Jesus Christ. The Apostle John speaks of the fear of punishment or torment (1 John 4:18) and that the perfect, whole and complete love of God drives out such fear. Paul also speaks of victory over fear when he states that nothing can separate us from the love of God (Romans 8:39). Separation from the love of God is the ultimate basis for fear. Death has been defeated and the cause of separation has been eternally removed in Christ – the foundation for fear has been undone. This is truth but truth that needs quite a bit of working into the fabric of our lives that may have been very accustomed to fear.

So was Jesus a bit harsh on His men or is this question offering the opportunity for some significant growth? As we allow Jesus to ask us this same question it can be an invitation to explore the deeper reasons for our fears, for why we get intimidated, why we hold back and hesitate at times. Jesus was present with the disciples in the storm. He is present with us and we can dare to confront our deepest and darkest fears in the Presence of Jesus. He invites us to be more impressed with Him than we are intimidated by what has sought to engulf us.

It is interesting that even as Jesus confronts their fear in the storm the disciples are moved to an even stronger fear at His authority to calm the wind and waves. Mark 5:41 states that they 'feared exceedingly.' They feared in response to experiencing an act of authority over nature's destructive power the likes of which they could never have imagined. This was a healthy fear that would not intimidate them but eventually release them into feats of faith and acts of authority themselves.

It is the love of God which is demonstrated in Christ that casts out all fear. It is faith in Christ that enables us to move past our timidity and life's intimidations, and releases and empowers us to slay giants and still storms. God understands our disposition and natural inclination to fear at times, yet He calls us to be strong and very courageous as He is with us wherever we go.

13

Is your heart still hardened?

Mark 8:17

Jesus was taking His disciples on an increasingly miraculous adventure. It wasn't just about the miracles themselves, nor was it for the disciples to be mere observers of Jesus' mighty works. Along this road Jesus was always looking to challenge and change the way these men thought, to stretch their understanding, enabling them to become true participants in God's Kingdom realm as it manifested on earth.

Throughout the previous chapters of Mark's dynamic and fast-paced account of the life of Jesus we see a series of miracles of healing, in chapter five, incredible feats of multiplying food and walking on water in chapter six, followed by more demonstrations of the Kingdom in chapter seven as the deaf hear and mute speak. Chapter eight brings another miraculous multiplication of food leading us to this discussion and questioning that we will examine now. A key statement throughout these events is found in Mark 6:52 explaining that they had not gained any insight from the incident with the loaves, but their hearts were hardened.

The incident with the loaves was the feeding of the 5,000 which was soon followed by an even more staggering event as Jesus comes to His disciples walking on the water. They couldn't get their heads around this; they were terrified and utterly astonished because they had gained no understanding from what they had seen previously. Jesus was seeking to develop something of world-changing potential in them but there was a blockage – hardened hearts. The word 'hardened' refers to a callous; a thick covering that has grown over their understanding causing a dullness of thinking.

The conversation (Mark 8:13-21) between Jesus and the twelve begins around bread. Jesus, along with their involvement, has recently multiplied small amounts of bread to feed multitudes, and now the disciples are concerned that they only have one loaf with them for the journey! Into the discussion around bread, Jesus also introduces the concept of the leaven, the agent used to make bread rise. He warns them about the leaven or yeast of both the Pharisees and Herod, of human-defined religion and rule. Both the Pharisees, right before this incident, and Herod on another occasion (Luke 23:8) look for a sign from Jesus as a proof. Jesus isn't interested in giving infallible proofs but leading those with hearts to see on a journey of true discovery. Jesus is leading them into a God defined partnership and the very different rule of His Kingdom.

Leaven corresponds to influence and can be good or bad, life-giving or limiting. Here Jesus refers to a negative influence strongly warning His followers not to let it rise up in them. On another occasion, he speaks a parable of the powerful, unseen, good influence of the Kingdom of God within (Matthew 13:33). It is this leaven that Jesus is always looking to implant within His followers.

The disciples still don't get it and carry on discussing or reasoning among themselves within their own group and limited worldview. They are not yet expanding with the leaven of the Kingdom. Likewise, we can remain in the limitations of valuing human reason over spiritual revelation. Our power of reason is not to be dismissed but needs to be submitted to and superseded by the greater wisdom and revelation from the Spirit of God.

Jesus embarks on a series of questions exposing the dullness of their hearts and drawing them out and up into seeing something beyond their present understanding and putting together what has up to now been disjointed:

Do you not yet see or understand?
Do you have a hardened heart?
Do you not see? Do you not hear?
Do you not remember?
Do you not yet understand?

What is Jesus seeking to develop in you at this time? What is He looking for you to get hold of? Is your understanding influenced and defined by the wrong type of leaven?

Jesus refers His disciples back to the loaves of bread at the two miraculous feedings. They can answer these questions as they do remember the number of basketfuls of leftovers that they collected. He refers us back to what He has done in us, through us and with us. He refers us back to what we may have seen and then draws us forward that we might gain insight from that. And in all this conversation with us He is asking if we understand yet or are there things that are still blocking that from happening.

What causes our hearts to harden or become dull and calloused?

Maybe it is disappointments or offence, scepticism or cynicism, or mental strongholds. It can be little things – a word here and there – but together they form and build a covering that dulls down the sound of heaven. This hardening or forming of a callous can be a slow and almost unnoticeable process. We must 'guard our hearts' as the Proverb cautions us (Proverbs 4:23), not only from the responses to hurt that can lead down a path of self-pity or even bitterness, but also from any entrenched position that limits our vision.

What prevents us from truly understanding? Understanding means putting all the pieces together, seeing the whole picture, seeing it as Jesus sees it. Maybe struggling to get by, just surviving or being caught up with many things and therefore not taking time to remember, reflect and realise the greater work all contribute to a lack of understanding.

Jesus was and is inviting His followers into the increasing, expanding, miraculous adventure of the Kingdom of God. He wants us to gain insight from what has been so as to develop foresight of what could be in the realm where 'everything is possible for the one who believes.' A heart that remains supple and teachable will receive the fullest benefit from His implanted seed.

14

But who do you say that I am?

Mark 8:29

Jesus is always after hearts that are being opened to believe and receive the revelation of who He is and of the reality of His Kingdom. In the last question, we observed that our hearts can be dull and hardened thus preventing good reception. Something needs to happen within us to bring clarity of vision. We find this occurring in the short account of a blind man receiving sight in the verses between our last question and this current one (Mark 8:22-26).

A blind man is led by the hand to Jesus maybe by some friends or relatives. Jesus takes this man out of the village, away from any source of unbelief, before laying His hands on him. Jesus then asks a question: 'Do you see anything?' Amazingly the blind man now begins to see but his vision is somewhat blurred as he sees 'men like trees walking.' Jesus is neither satisfied with such a partial restoration, nor deterred by it, and once again places His hands on the man's eyes. Now the man sees everything clearly.

It may be that many of us have received sight from Jesus but that we are not seeing clearly. It may be that we are in need of another touch from the Redeemer and Restorer of all things, a touch that will bring truer revelation and fuller understanding of who Jesus is and what He is doing in bringing His Kingdom to come on earth as in heaven - a fresh touch that brings focus to the eyes of our hearts. Proverbs 4:18 says, 'the path of the righteous is like the light of dawn, that shines brighter and brighter until the full day'.

Jesus now takes His band of disciples to Caesarea Philippi, a city of Greek-Roman culture known for its worship of foreign gods, where He would reveal some key truths to them. He begins this process by asking the disciples two questions:
Who do people say that I am?
But who do you say that I am?
The first question was relatively easy to answer. The disciples had no doubt heard many people speculating and commenting on who this miracle worker from Nazareth was. Some say John the Baptist, others Elijah and others see Him as another one of the prophets. Now Jesus presses in and asks the most important question. He makes it personal – but what about you?

Why is this such an important question to answer? If we don't recognise who Jesus truly is then we can't fully receive what He gives to us. If we don't understand who Jesus fully is then we can't receive the fullness of identity that can only be found in relation to Him. Our answer to this question is vital. The answer will develop as we grow into a fuller recognition of all that He is - the greater appreciation of His Name. We may start with an appreciation of Jesus as Saviour, growing into the understanding of Him as Lord, as Redeemer, as Shepherd and much more. Very importantly the answer is revealed to us from the Father, as Jesus states in Matthew 16:17:

"Flesh and blood did not reveal this to you, but My Father who is in heaven."

And again in Matthew 11:27:

"No one knows the Son except the Father; nor does anyone know the Father except the Son, and anyone to whom the Son wills to reveal Him."

It is not an answer we can get second hand from others. It is not something we reason out. It is not an answer of our own making.

Jesus points His question to each of us – 'never mind what everyone else is saying, what about you?' What is being revealed to you? Who do you say that I am? Not just a good, sound theological answer, important as that is, but who am I personally to you? Not merely knowing about Him, but knowing Him.

It is a question some believers may feel they have answered some time ago. Yet the light 'shines brighter and brighter till the full day'. In one way Peter's answer was sufficient, 'You are the Christ'. Yet there is more to discover of the fullness of the Christ. Paul prays that we would be given 'the spirit of wisdom and revelation in the knowledge of Him' and that 'the eyes of our hearts would be enlightened.' He never changes but our appreciation of who He is can develop.

Our answer becomes a building block for further revelation and teaching from the Lord. Matthew's account shows how Jesus takes Peter's response and builds something more of deep importance and significance on that (Matthew 16:17-19). Our recognition and confession of who Jesus is provides a platform for Him to reveal more of the identity He gives to us and the purpose He has for us.

15

What were you arguing about?

Mark 9:33 (NIV)

The band of twelve disciples was a mixed bunch brought together by the call of a Rabbi who they would discover to be the Son of the Living God. Some knew each other beforehand, some were brothers, some had the same occupation, and others came from quite different backgrounds. Encountering Jesus and responding to His call brought a great shift in their lives. They would spend time with Him but also significant time with each other. What would they have chatted about as they walked along the dusty roads from village to village? They might have talked and wondered together about the miracles they witnessed. They certainly discussed some of Jesus' sayings, especially those they did not yet understand.

These men had been chosen, and as they listened to the wise and authoritative teaching, watched the healings and miracles, and the astonished and amazed crowds, they must have felt quite privileged to be in the inner circle. Then they had been sent out and they themselves healed the sick and cast out demons. Three of them, however, seemed to get preferential treatment. Only Peter, James and John accompany Jesus as He raises Jairus' daughter from the dead. The same three are invited up to the mountain where Jesus is transfigured and the Father's voice is heard speaking from the cloud. How did that make those three feel? How did it affect the other nine?

Those other nine are left in the valley while Jesus and the three ascend the mountain. During this time a father brings his troubled and mute son to these disciples to have them cast out the tormenting spirit and heal the boy (Mark 9:14-29). They had previously been sent out in two's and had cast out demons – they knew the authority Jesus gave to them. But on this occasion, they are unable to bring the needed deliverance and healing. This leads to an argument with the religious scribes who were seizing the opportunity to question His followers. Inability to demonstrate the power and authority of the Lord will often reduce His people to arguments.

Jesus asks, maybe of the scribes, or His disciples, or both, what they were discussing and arguing about? No one answers but the distraught father who is desperately seeking a cure for his disturbed son. Jesus, wondering at the unbelief that surrounds Him, sets the boy free and restores him to his father. From here Mark tells us they went out and started going throughout Galilee. They had time on the journeys to ponder these events but they also get into discussions, arguing about which one of them is the greatest!

Maybe it was the special experiences of the three, the apparent failure of the others to heal the boy, or simply their insecurities that lead them into this spirit of comparison and competition. It is one we are all familiar with. Our world operates a system of comparison and competition – in business, in sport, in beauty and in life in general. We've all been schooled in it to a degree.

Why do we compare ourselves and who with?
What do we compete for? Who do we compete with?
Why do we compete?
Jesus asks us, 'What are you arguing about?'

Like the disciples, we may compete for position, for prominence, and for recognition, and to feel more significant about ourselves in comparison to those around us. We can even feel better about ourselves when others fail or struggle.

What does this contending lead to?

It may lead us into striving to perform and the wearying demand to keep up this performance. It may subtly drive us to exaggerate ourselves and our achievements, to add a little, or a whole load of spin in order to look better. Such pretence eventually cracks.

Job asks a question of his companions and supposed comforters:

"What ails you that you keep on arguing?" (Job 16:3 NIV).

What grieves or pains or plagues us that we fall into the grip of comparing and competing? Is it fear of other people getting ahead of us, of being rewarded more than us, or of appearing more significant and important than we are?

Jesus asks, 'What were you arguing about?'

His question silences the disciples for they are exposed by it and embarrassed at the nature of their discussion. Jesus uses the opportunity of the moment to impart a key Kingdom principle to His men – the first shall be last and the last shall be first. It's not about prominence and position. It's not about you, but about who you represent.

Jesus redeems us from under the Law with its slavery to judgement, and entitles and enables us to receive true Sonship and live in its benefits (see Galatians 4:4-7). True sons and daughters of the True Father don't need to judge and compare themselves to anyone else for they are being formed into the likeness of His Son (Romans 8:29). We no longer 'regard anyone (including ourselves) according to the flesh' but see the new creation (2 Corinthians 5:16-17). We are no longer forced to compete for limited rewards but enjoy the limitless resources and favour of our Father's Kingdom. Free from competition we can fight the real battles and focus on the main task together.

As children of God, secured in His covenant love, we are freed from the spirit of comparison and competition, no longer ruled by the opinions of other people. As representatives of Jesus Christ, we have true and eternal significance no longer needing to vie for recognition or reward. As His chosen ones we can live in and enjoy His favour – and there is more than enough to go around.

16

What do you want Me to do for you?

Mark 10:51

A large, bustling crowd moved slowly along the road out of Jericho. The air was filled with the dust from their footsteps and a sense of anticipation and wonder at the One they were following. By the roadside sat Bartimaeus, a blind man begging for alms. He could have been easily missed in the encompassing excitement and enveloping sounds, and was comfortably dismissed as of no importance by those in the busy throng.

What was going through Bartimaeus' mind? He couldn't see what was happening but he could hear the commotion and could feel the highly charged atmosphere. Then he hears that it is Jesus of Nazareth who is passing by on His way out of town. He has no doubt heard the reports of the lame walking, the deaf hearing and yes, the blind seeing. This is his day, his opportunity and he is not going to let it slip away. He cries out, "Jesus, Son of David, have mercy on me!" Not once but again and again. Some in the crowd resent his disturbing cries and rebuke him telling him to be quiet. But Bartimaeus has glimpsed the possibility of this moment and he will let no one silence him and steal this from him as he shouts out even louder.

Amazingly Jesus stops and calls for Bartimaeus, this poor blind beggar. Suddenly those in the fickle crowd change their tone and encourage Bartimaeus to get up and go to Jesus. Bartimaeus leaps to his feet, throwing aside his cloak and presents himself before Jesus who has heard his call for mercy. Jesus now wants to get specific about the mercy that Bartimaeus is crying out for and asks the question: What do you want Me to do for you? What an invitation and maybe a challenge too. He could just have been looking for some money or for Jesus to tell the people to look after him. Jesus gives him the opportunity to express his desire and the dignity of not presuming what he needs. Bartimaeus' response is as straightforward and clear as the question – "I want to see!"

What do you want Me to do for you? Let Jesus ask you that question right now. How does that feel? Is there a straight answer like this blind man gives or do you want to ponder this for a while? What do you really want to ask Jesus for?

Yet sometimes we are afraid to ask and afraid to answer this question. Why? Maybe the rumblings of past disappointment resound in our memories when we asked but didn't appear to receive. Then there's the derailing effect of false humility or the nagging noise of doubt, or maybe we simply don't know what we really want. There's also that sentiment that other people have greater needs than me as if God had a limited supply that He has to carefully guard in case it runs out. Maybe He wants to give us more than we ask or think or imagine.

Jesus had asked this very same question earlier in this chapter in Mark 10:36, but in an entirely different context and with a very different answer. Two of His inner circle, the brothers James and John, had come to Jesus with a request that He do for them whatever they ask. Well, they certainly had bold faith. So Jesus asks them, "What do you want Me to do for you?" They answer that they want the best seats, an answer borne from pride, presumption and a degree of selfishness. Bartimaeus had answered Jesus question out of an acute awareness of his need and with a cry for mercy.

Jesus has recently been teaching the principles of His upside-down Kingdom where the first will be last and the last will be first. He had not long ago caught out His disciples arguing over which of them was the greatest, and immediately before they make their request He has been speaking of His sacrificial death. The pretentious answer from these brothers shows they have embraced very little of what Jesus has been telling them. Jesus won't grant them those special seats – they are not His to assign – but will answer them by once again relating the values of His Kingdom where the first among you shall be the slave of all, and that He Himself did not come to be served but to serve.

To ask for something is not being selfish but recognising our need. Jesus encourages us to ask, to seek and to knock; to come shamelessly to God for what we lack. But does He always answer? In His teaching about prayer in Luke 11:1-13 Jesus gives us a model for praying, a parable to embolden us to press through the barriers, and a clue to the way God answers prayer. That answer is the Holy Spirit:

"How much more will your heavenly Father give the Holy Spirit to those who ask Him?" (Luke 11:13)
How is He the answer? The Spirit takes all that is Christ's and makes it known to us – His righteousness, love, peace, joy, healing and much more.

Bartimaeus knew that he needed mercy and that Jesus had it to give. This blind man kept it simple and he knew what he truly desired – to see! He expressed his need, he refused to be silenced, he believed and received his sight, and followed Jesus along the road.

17

Are you still sleeping?

Mark 14:41

It was the most difficult, demanding and decisive time. Jesus was moving headlong into the fulfilment of what He had prophesied about Himself, that He would be betrayed, arrested, tried, mocked, scourged and put to death. As He enters the Garden of Gethsemane Jesus is going through deep distress and agonising anguish of soul. He is looking for His friends and followers to support Him and keep watch. He leaves most of the group at one point while once again taking His inner circle of Peter, James, and John a little further with Him. Jesus then goes a little beyond them to pour out the depths of His soul before His Father. Returning to the three men Jesus finds them sleeping. A pattern follows of Jesus going and praying and then finding them asleep once more. He questions them and they really don't know what to say in response. They just couldn't stay awake, alert and keep watch, not even for one hour.

I think we can often identify with these drowsy disciples. We set ourselves to pray and to seek the Lord only to find ourselves feeling weary and overcome by tiredness. So what is it that is at work causing this slumbering to fall on us? Why could Peter, James, and John not keep awake at the crucial hour? Why is Jesus needing to ask, 'Are you still sleeping?'

Sleep is good for us; it is even a gift from God:

"For He grants sleep to those He loves" (Psalm 127:2 NIV).

Sleep is a great benefit to us physically, emotionally, mentally and spiritually. God often meets with people in the night through dreams and other encounters. Jesus isn't questioning the need for and value of sleep. He is not scolding His disciples for being lazy, but He is looking for alertness in the spirit and an awakening to the greater realities going on around us. Alertness, watchfulness, and prayer go together:

"Devote yourselves to prayer, keeping alert in it" (Colossians 4:2).

And there is a battle – in the spiritual realm and with our own flesh life.

These men's eyes were 'very heavy' (Mark 14:40) and on another occasion, it says that the same three men were 'overcome (or heavy) with sleep' (Luke 9:32). Luke's account of the Gethsemane experience tells us

that they were 'sleeping from sorrow' (Luke 22:45).
Why was this?

They are entering Jesus' darkest hour with Him having
been forewarned that things are going to get a lot
worse before they get better. They are naturally
sorrowful. Sorrow, grief, and pressures weigh heavily on
our emotions infiltrating into our bodily capacities. This
heaviness can have many causes from the various
weights we carry. These may come from the numerous
concerns of life; the disappointments of the past,
discouragement in the present or worry for the future.
Isaiah describes this 'spirit of heaviness' which is literally
'a fainting spirit' and also offers us an antidote in the
'garment of praise.' (Isaiah 61:3). To the sorrowful,
those who mourn He offers 'the oil of gladness.'

Are you still sleeping? Or are you alert and keeping
watch? What is bringing heaviness to your eyes? Are
you overcome at times by a slumbering in your soul?
How do we overcome being overcome with this sleepy,
fainting spirit?

Several antidotes and remedies are provided but we
need to take hold of these, put them on and apply them
in our lives:

The oil of gladness: Joy brings a wonderful refreshing to us, even releasing health to our bodies. This joy is based in the Lord, in who He is, the hope He gives, in His promises and presence. We may not always feel it but we can always choose to rejoice. Rejoicing is not something that comes upon us but an activity that we engage in by an act of our will. David declared, 'I will be glad and rejoice in You' (Psalm 9:2). Paul emphasises to 'Rejoice in the Lord, and again I say, rejoice!' (Philippians 4:4). Isaiah relates a further prophetic promise from God that there will joy and rejoicing in the house of prayer (Isaiah 56:7).

The garment of praise: This joy of and in the Lord leads into songs of praise (see Psalm 9:2). Joy filled people sing. The garment of praise needs to be picked up and put on as we declare and sing of the glorious attributes of God. Such praise shifts the heaviness and the high praises of God bind up the works of darkness (see Psalm 149:5-9). Paul and Silas, in a dark dungeon, could easily have been overcome with heaviness, but instead, put on the garment of praise resulting in prison doors springing open and chains breaking loose (Acts 16:25-26).

Casting over anxiety: Both Peter and Paul encourage us to cast away and give over to God the wearying weights of worry and anxious thoughts:

"Casting all your anxiety on Him, because He cares for you" (1 Peter 5:7)

"Be anxious for nothing, but in everything by prayer and supplication with thanksgiving let your requests be made known to God" (Philippians 4:6).

Paul sets this in the context of prayer encouraging us to release what causes us anxiety alongside a healthy dose of thankfulness to the God who cares for us. This, he announces, will bring to us a peace that is beyond the limited understanding of our finite minds; a peace that truly guards our hearts and minds against distraction, discouragement and drowsiness.

Seeing His glory: On the mountain where Jesus is transfigured and meets with Moses and Elijah, those three privileged disciples, Peter, James, and John, again become heavy and overcome with sleep (Luke 9:32). Maybe it was the long, steep climb but they couldn't keep their eyes open. Then like the morning sunshine glistening through the curtains, they are awakened from their slumber. Becoming fully awake, like opening wide the curtains to the full brightness of the sun, they see and behold His glory.

Are you still sleeping? Are your eyes heavy? It's time to wake up, rise up and let Christ Jesus shine on you. There is glory to behold and to be fully awakened to its life-transforming effects.

18

What are you seeking?

John 1:38 (ESV)

John the Baptist had been called to prepare the way for the One who was coming after him. He wasn't the Messiah but was to point others to Him. His was a ministry of graciously pointing away from himself, and even steering his own followers to leave him and go and follow Jesus. John had got a revelation; he had seen a glimpse of who Jesus really was – the Lamb of God! Twice we read of John declaring publicly and encouraging those around to behold, to see, to look upon this greater One. On the second occasion two of John's own disciples are present, and on hearing this they begin to follow after Jesus. Turning and seeing them walking behind Him, Jesus asks this question, 'What are you seeking?'

What are you seeking? What are you looking for? What are you really after?

People come to Jesus for a variety of initial reasons. Though drawn invisibly by the Holy Spirit, we come looking for different things – forgiveness, a new start, purpose in life, freedom, healing, and much more. As we walk with Him, His influence affects our desires, refining and developing our search. What were you seeking when you first encountered Jesus? What are you seeking now? Our original seeking may have been very much for our personal benefit, and rightly so at that stage, but then develops into something greater as Jesus calls us to 'seek first the Kingdom of God and His righteousness' with the promise that in doing so all else we need will be amply supplied.

The two disciples answer Jesus' question with a question – 'where are you staying?' Maybe they weren't yet sure what they were seeking as they had just felt the impulse to respond to their previous Rabbi's announcement. They were intrigued to discover more of whom this 'Lamb of God' truly was and what He was all about. Jesus invites them to come and see, and they spend the day with Him. Andrew, one of these two young men, was so impressed with Jesus that he goes off and finds his brother, Simon, and immediately introduces him to Jesus.

What are you seeking? What are you really after at this season of your life? Or have you grown tired or complacent and the search has ground to a halt?

Jesus encourages us to ask, to seek and to knock with the promise that as we continue to do so we will receive, find and have doors opened to us (Luke 11:9-10). Seeking begins with desire and leads to direction. David says that he desires one thing and this is therefore what he will seek:

"One thing I have desired of the LORD,
That will I seek" (Psalm 27:4 NKJV).

There is a need to ask ourselves about what we truly do desire. As this unfolds and dawns within us then the seeking commences leading us on the adventure of discovery. We cannot do this half-heartedly. Scripture counsels us to 'seek the Lord with all our heart' (Jeremiah 29:13) if we are to find Him and His fulfilling purposes for us.

What are you seeking? Will you 'spend the day' with Jesus so that He can make His imprint on your heart forming His greater intentions into your desires? He will not lead you on some forlorn search for mystical treasure that you will never find, but He will usher you forward and accompany you to the true treasures of His Kingdom. He will guide you on a glorious search for that which His Father and your Father is delighted to bring to fruitful fulfilment.

19

Do you want to be made well?

John 5:6 (NIV)

For a long number of years he had been by this mysterious pool, along with a large number of others who were similarly crippled. Sitting, waiting, hoping, and getting discouraged and losing hope of anything ever happening for him, of ever being healed. Yet still he is waiting, maybe more out of habit than expectation. He had played the scenes in his mind, the possibilities that never came about, and now all he seemed to have was his self-pity.

Jesus appears on the scene directing His gaze on this one man among many who were in need of healing. Knowing that the man had been in this condition a long time Jesus asks him, 'Do you want to be made well?' What would he reply? 'Oh yes, of course, that's what I've been waiting and longing for all these years.' He neither says 'yes' or 'no' but begins to relate his long-rehearsed excuses formed through years of disappointment. The sick man is only viewing one option for being made well, and that is being first in the pool after the next stirring of the waters. Jesus has something altogether different in mind.

Do you want to be made well, sound of body and whole? Do you want to live in good health? Who wouldn't? Yet … not everyone appears to or else why would Jesus ask this question at all?

Like this man in the story, we can be trapped in the miserable yet strangely comforting clutch of self-pity. We can be looking for sympathy believing that it brings a true reward. But Jesus never came to sympathise though He does come full of compassion. There is a clear and marked difference. Sympathy comes into an agreement with the condition and suffering, furthering their subtle hold. Compassion (the Biblical word can also be translated as indignation) means a deep moving in the guts that leads to action that brings about redemption, remedy, and release.

The length of time this man had been sick, thirty-eight long years, may have even resulted in him befriending this condition. It was all he now knew, all he could remember, it was the focus of his days, and it had taken on a place of familiarity and even identity in his life. He had been blinded to how it had robbed him.

So the answer to Jesus' question isn't so straightforward. There are many complications and conflicting thoughts within the human heart. Do you want to be made well? What will that mean? What will you have to relinquish? What might change? The question isn't straightforward because the causes and conditions of being unwell are many and varied. It is not simply about physical restoration, but the healing of the sometimes complex damage within our souls. Jesus' question isn't limited to those who are bodily crippled in some form but the often unseen crippling of mind, will and emotions.

Another issue for this sick man, and maybe others like him, is the fear of having their hopes raised only to be dashed once more. Healing may have seemed elusive. It may have happened for other people like those who got down the steps into the pool first. Jesus doesn't focus on those others, but directs His eyes and words to this one, commanding him to get up and walk – and he does! He even got the strength to pick up his pallet and carry that which had carried him for so long. He was free from that sickness and free from his excuses, and it was now time for him to step up.

Do you want to be made well? Or have you become so accustomed to some crippling limitations in your life that you have justified and simply accepted their hindering presence? Maybe it has been a long time and you have got by just fine. You have coped, and that seems quite admirable. You don't need any help or anyone to do something for you. Yet Jesus – the Healer, the Redeemer, and the Saviour – asks the question. The punishment that brings us well-being was laid on Him, and by His wounds we are healed (Isaiah 53:5; 1 Peter 2:24). His question invites us, and at the same time challenges us into receiving something He paid for on our behalf. We have to admit we need Jesus to do something for us, that only He can truly make us whole.

20

Do you love Me?

John 21:15-17

The last time Simon saw Jesus alive he was standing by
a charcoal fire having denied Him for the third time.
After all the amazing experiences, the miracles and
revelation of the last few years he ends up denying that
he even knows Jesus. The rooster crows and he's blown
it! He had been so sure he wouldn't ever deny Jesus
even if all the other disciples did (see Mark 14:29-31).
He runs out and weeps bitterly, his soul torn in torment
with grief and shame. It might have been a tragic
ending, but Jesus is raised from death and presents
Himself alive to His followers. Simon and the other
disciples rejoiced even if they were somewhat
bewildered. And yet is Simon wondering? What might
Jesus say about His denials?

John's Gospel tells us that Jesus appears twice to His
disciples in the room where they were hiding out of fear
that they might be next for crucifixion. But Jesus doesn't
say anything specific to Simon. The third time Jesus
appears is back to a scene familiar to where a number

of them encountered Him for the first time, and where He called them to follow. They are fishing, and like on a previous occasion without any success (Luke 5:1-11). A word from the Lord changes everything and there's another miraculous catch! Added to the scene by the shores this time is a charcoal fire. The scene is set for something most significant.

The fishermen recognise that it's Jesus, and Simon Peter leaps enthusiastically into the water to get there first. They bring up the laden nets and it's time for breakfast. After they have finished eating Jesus directs this question to Simon, 'Do you love Me more than these?' This could equally mean, 'do you love Me more than these others do?' or 'do you love Me more than you love them?' Simon's response no longer contains the sort of boast he had previously made, but humbly recognises Jesus' knowledge of him and that Simon indeed does love Him even though he has stumbled. The question is repeated in a shorter form, simply asking, 'Do you love Me?' Simon gives an identical response. Then comes the same question a third penetrating time, 'Do you love Me?' Simon can't fail to see the link to his previous three denials by a charcoal fire. And yet this is not a rebuke or an accusation, but a restoration. Simon Peter doesn't need to be reinstated as he was never dismissed, but he does need to be restored in his own mind and heart, and in the presence of the others. The restoration is made complete by a threefold commissioning to feed and tend the lambs and sheep of Christ the Good Shepherd.

To those who have stumbled, who feel they have failed and are now failures; to those who have even denied knowing Jesus there is hope and there is restoration. But true restoration needs to search and reach deep into the heart. Jesus' questions to Simon in this setting bring up painful memories of his foolhardy boasting, and rash and cowardly denials. This isn't a smooth glossing over. That would not satisfy and heal the scarring of Simon's soul. The third asking of the same question causes Simon to grieve and to feel sorrow. Jesus exposes the depths in order to apply His healing balm, to revitalise and re-establish Simon. There may be pain in the process of restoration.

Why did Jesus ask this question to Simon and why does He ask it of us today? He could have asked Simon a number of other questions: Will you be a faithful witness now, even under threat? Will you ever deny Me again? Have you learned your lesson about making boastful claims? But no, Jesus asks, 'Do you love Me?'

Jesus is after our hearts and a response of love to the love that He has shown us. This is the ultimate question of relationship. Simon Peter was restored in the perfect love of His Lord, and because of this love, he does remain a faithful witness even under threat and imprisonment. He never does deny Jesus again, not even when he too is put to death.

Jesus asks, 'Do you love Me?' John tells us elsewhere:
"We love because He first loved us" (1 John 4:19). Are you receiving and understanding His love for you? He is after our hearts, our love not our performance. As we love Him so we will delightfully obey Him. We are designed to be loved and to love, to share in the love of the Godhead. Jesus said:
"I have made Your name known to them, and will make it known, so that the love with which You loved Me may be in them, and I in them" (John 17:26).
He then tasks us with feeding and tending to others, not because we have to out of a driven sense of duty, but because we love Him and therefore love who He loves.

About the Author

Steven Anderson has been involved in a variety of Christian leadership roles since 1987. Steven was pastor of Castlemilk Baptist Church in Glasgow from 1987 - 1999, before he, and his wife Helen, together formed Prayer for the City in Glasgow, a ministry seeking to bring united, envisioned and sustained prayer for transformation. In 2004 they pioneered Healing Rooms in Scotland which they led as National Directors for 10 years, seeing over 50 rooms open and operating across the nation.

They have been involved in church planting, street ministry among homeless people in their city, ministry in prisons, training and mentoring, and have ministered in several nations especially Ukraine.
In 2016 they moved to England where Steven became Senior Leader of Biggleswade Baptist Church in Bedfordshire until returning to Scotland in 2018.
They have written several books including *Breakthrough Prayer, Releasing Healing* and *The Day That Changed My Life.*

Contact Information:

E-mail: stevenjohnanderson1@gmail.com

Printed in Great Britain
by Amazon